JULIA BUTTERFLY HILL

DAWN FITZGERALD

JULIA BUTTERFLY HILL

Saving the Redwoods

A Gateway Green Biography
The Millbrook Press
Brookfield, Connecticut

Dedicated to my children, Ryan and Brynn

Cover photograph courtesy of © Shaun Walker

Photographs courtesy of © Shaun Walker: pp. 6, 8, 22, 23, 25, 28, 29, 33, 37, 38, 39, 42;
© Gustavo Gilabert/SABA: p. 11; The Image Works: pp. 13 (© Andrew Lichtenstein), 15 (©
Michael Thompson), 19 (© Andrew Lichtenstein); Visuals Unlimited: p. 17 (© D. Long);
AP/Wide World Photos: pp. 18, 21, 35; © John Storey/TimePix: p. 31

Library of Congress Cataloging-in-Publication Data
FitzGerald, Dawn.
Julia Butterfly Hill : saving the redwoods / Dawn FitzGerald.
p. cm. – (Gateway green)
Includes bibliographical references (p.).
Summary: Describes how Julia Butterfly Hill lived for two years in a California redwood tree in
an attempt to save the forest from loggers.
ISBN 0-7613-2654-5 (lib. bdg.)
1. Hill, Julia Butterfly—Juvenile literature. 2. Women conservationists—California—Humboldt
County—Biography—Juvenile literature. 3. Luna (Calif. : Tree)—Juvenile literature. 4. Old
growth forest conservation—California—Humboldt County—Juvenile literature. 5. Logging—
California—Humboldt County—Juvenile literature. 6. Pacific Lumber Company—Juvenile literature. [1. Hill, Julia Butterfly. 2. Conservationists. 3. Coast redwood. 4. Forest conservation.] I.
Title. II. Gateway green biography.
SD129.H53 F58 2002
333.75'16'092—dc21 [B] 2001044921

Published by The Millbrook Press, Inc.
2 Old New Milford Road
Brookfield, Connecticut 06804
www.millbrookpress.com

JULIA BUTTERFLY HILL

Julia Butterfly Hill

Never doubt that a small group of thoughtful, committed citizens can change the world. Indeed, it's the only thing that ever has. —Margaret Mead

Up a Tree

One hundred and eighty feet (55 meters) high in the air, a young woman clings to a California redwood tree. It's raining very hard, and with every gust of wind the small platform she is on bucks and rocks like a wild horse. Tree branches crash to the forest floor. The girl turns her face from the cold rain and cries, "I can't do this anymore!"[1]

But it's too late. She cannot climb down the tree in the middle of the storm. Julia Butterfly Hill has no choice but to hang on for her life.

When Julia was a little girl, she once hid with her family in a cellar during a tornado. Strong winds twisted above their heads. Yet she felt safe underground with her parents and two brothers.

This time there is nobody to hold her. Nobody to tell her that everything will be all right. Julia hugs the redwood tree named Luna and tries to feel brave.

*Julia sits high in the branches of
her favorite redwood tree, Luna.*

After all, Luna has survived many storms in her lifetime. Luna's sturdy trunk is 15 feet (4.5 meters) wide at the base. At the top of her canopy there is a black scar from lightning that struck over one hundred years ago.

Julia opens her eyes and watches the giant trees of the forest swaying with the powerful winds. She feels Luna rocking back and forth.

Suddenly, Julia has an idea. She will move like the trees. If she holds her body stiff, the wind will snap her like a twig. But if she bends like the trees, she will survive and keep her promise to Luna.

What did Julia promise the thousand-year-old redwood? Like many trees in this forest, Luna has a blue X painted on her trunk. This X means that very soon the logging company will cut Luna down. The wood from Luna's trunk will be made into decks, picnic tables, and chairs.

Julia climbed into Luna's branches to save her. She hoped that the loggers would not cut down a tree with a person sitting in it. Julia was willing to stand up (or sit down) for her beliefs. But she hadn't planned on living in the tree for two years!

A Childhood on the Road

How do you prepare for living in a tree? If you had a childhood like Julia's, you would have learned many skills that would help you survive.

She learned at a very early age to make anywhere home. Her father was a traveling preacher and he did not stay very long at each church. Instead, he went from town to town, bringing his family along with him. In fact, Julia was born in the back of a bakery truck on February 18, 1974.

Until she was about ten years old, Julia lived in a 32-foot (10-meter) camper with her father, mother, and two younger brothers. The tiny camper was crowded. Yet living, eating, and sleeping in cramped conditions turned out to be perfect training for a future tree-sitter.

Julia's family was poor. She never had many toys or clothes. While other children her age watched cartoons and commercials on television, Julia explored rivers by their campgrounds. She studied the colors in stained-glass church windows as she listened to her father preach and the choir sing.

When Julia was five, she didn't start school like other children her age. Instead, her parents home-schooled their children. The camper and the world around it became Julia's classroom. She learned to read, write, and work math problems inside the camper. But her favorite lessons took place outside. In the campgrounds, she and her brothers explored the woods, climbed trees, and met people from all over the country.

The Hill family enjoyed hiking in forests. When Julia was six years old, an amazing thing happened during a hike. A monarch butterfly landed on her finger and rested there as she walked the trails of the forest. Her brothers couldn't believe that the butterfly didn't fly away. It remained with Julia during the entire hike. From that day on, her nickname was Butterfly.

Julia has admired butterflies ever since she was a child when one landed on her finger and stayed there during a long hike.

When Julia was in middle school, her family stopped traveling and settled in Arkansas. Julia and her brothers attended public school.

The strict school schedule and new rules were confining. She missed being close to nature and having the freedom to explore her interests.

When Julia was in the eleventh grade, some students smashed other students' cars with baseball bats. Everyone in school knew who did it, but nobody had the courage to tell. They were afraid that the bullies would come after them.

Julia spoke out against the bullies even though she knew she might get hurt. She figured that the bullies would continue hurting people if she kept silent and did nothing.

After graduating from high school, Julia went to college for two years. She worked at two jobs to help pay for school. She modeled for a clothing catalog and worked in a restaurant. Although her life was very busy with work and classes, Julia felt it lacked direction. She had no idea what she wanted to study or what type of job she wanted after college.

One day while driving home from work, Julia stopped at a red light. A pickup truck behind her crashed into her small car and her head slammed into the steering wheel. She spent many weeks in the hospital. After she returned home, it took her ten months to recover from the accident.

When she felt better, Julia decided to search for a purpose in her life. Where could she make a difference? How could she make every single moment count? Julia wanted to see all of the beauty in the world, so she took a year off from school to travel.

Three of Julia's close friends were planning a trip to Washington State to see Mount Olympia Rain Forest. Julia had never seen this part of the country, so she went with them. But she never made it to Mount Olympia. The purpose she had been searching for came to her along the way.

A forest of ancient redwood trees in California. The redwoods, along with the sequoia and the Douglas fir, are the oldest and tallest living things on Earth. The redwoods grow only in the Pacific Northwest.

Meeting the Redwoods

On their way to Mount Olympia, Julia and her friends stopped to see the giant redwood trees in Humboldt County, California. No one on the trip had ever seen redwoods before.

In her autobiography, *The Legacy of Luna*, Julia describes the first time she walked in the redwood forest: "As I headed farther into the forest, I could no longer hear the sounds of the cars or smell their fumes. I breathed in the pure, wonderful air. . . . For the first time I really felt what it was like to be alive, to feel the connection of all life."[2]

Julia stood before a grove of redwoods that towered over 200 feet (61 meters) high. She dropped to her knees in wonder, feeling respect and love for these very old trees.

Afterward, Julia saw posters showing how logging companies were cutting down the trees. The posters made her upset. She remembered how peaceful she felt in the forest, breathing in the redwood smell and feeling the mossy bark. Suddenly, she knew what she wanted to do—save the redwoods!

Her friends weren't surprised when she told them her plan. They knew they would not be able to change her mind. As her friends drove north, Julia found an environmental group and volunteered to help save the trees.

*It would take approximately fifteen people holding hands
to encircle the huge trunk of just one redwood tree.*

But the environmental group told Julia to go home. It didn't
need her help because winter was coming. There would not be
many marches or protests.

Julia was disappointed. With very little money and even less hope, she returned to her family in Arkansas. But her heart remained with the California redwoods.

Back home she felt sad. She remembered standing among the redwood trees and being part of the beauty and mystery around her. She couldn't forget the posters showing the destruction of forests. Besides, when had "no" ever stopped her before?

So Julia made a decision. She sold most of her belongings, keeping only a few photo albums, some artwork, and her violin. Using the money from the sale, she headed back to Humboldt County and the giant redwoods.

Battle Lines

Julia walked in on more than a simple disagreement when she returned to the redwoods. She entered a war zone. The Pacific Lumber Company and the environmental activists were battling over cutting down old-growth trees.

Loggers use chainsaws 6 feet (1.8 meters) long to cut down trees on company property. After this clear-cutting, the ground is barren. Nothing remains where once thousand-year-old trees grew in ancient forests.

Clear-cutting forests decreases habitats for endangered animals and plants. When giant logs are dragged to the logging

*A forest that has been clear-cut can no longer
shelter all the plants and animals that lived there.*

trucks, the soil is disturbed. Dirt and silt run into the streams
and rivers. This makes it impossible for endangered fish, like
the Coho salmon, to live and breed.

The extensive damage from the Stafford, California, mudslide is shown here. The mudslide destroyed houses and other property. Later, the residents filed a lawsuit against the lumber company for irresponsible logging practices.

Clear-cutting trees affects human homes, too. In 1996, in Stafford, California, a giant mudslide covered seven homes.[3] Cutting trees from a hillside wrecks the root system that holds soil and rocks in place and absorbs water when it rains. After heavy rains, the dirt turns to thick mud and rolls down the mountainside.

Environmental activists try to slow the rate of logging and preserve the old-growth forests. Activists give speeches, march at rallies, and hand out flyers about their cause.

Logging companies provide lumber that is used to build homes, furniture, and many other wood products we use every day.

Tree-sits are the most difficult way to save a tree. Julia Butterfly Hill said, "Tree-sitting is a last resort."[4] A tree-sitter thinks, "I have no other way to stop what's happening. I have no other way to make people aware of what's at stake. . . . So it's my responsibility to give this one last shot, to put my body where my beliefs are."[5]

Tree-sitting is dangerous and often fails. Logging companies have cut down trees with tree-sitters still in the branches. The tree-sitter is forced to climb down quickly or jump before the tree crashes to the ground.

Julia knew very little about the struggle between the Pacific Lumber Company and the environmental activists. All she knew is that she wanted to help. At a meeting, an activist named Almond asked if anyone would tree-sit for a few days to give another tree-sitter a break. Julia raised her hand in a flash.

As they walked to the tree-sit, Almond explained that she would need a forest name. All activists adopt code names to avoid trouble. The only name Julia could think of was her childhood nickname, Butterfly. But butterflies are delicate and she wanted a name that showed bravery and strength.

Then she remembered the butterfly that had rested on her finger when she was a little girl. Even a small butterfly shows great strength in leaving the place where it was born and flying

Hundreds of people protest logging in front of the Pacific Lumber Company in 1996.

over 1,000 miles (1,609 kilometers) to a winter home. Julia knew what it was like to take a chance and follow her heart.

"Do you have a forest name?"[6] Almond asked as they hiked to the tree.

Julia answered, "Butterfly."

The tree-sitting platform was 8 feet (2.4 m) long and 6 feet (1.8 m) wide, about as large as a queen-size bed. It sat 180 feet (55 m) high in the branches.

A Promise

On the misty morning when Julia saw Luna for the first time, the tops of the branches and trunk were hidden by fog. Redwoods are sometimes called cloudsweepers for this reason.

The tree-sitting platform had been built in 1997 from plywood and nailed down by activists. They worked late at night by the light of a harvest moon. "Luna" is the Spanish word for the moon. This giant redwood, perched at the edge of a steep cliff, has been called Luna ever since.

Now Julia had to learn how to climb the tree with ropes. She was buckled into an old harness held together with duct tape. She practiced how to grip the ropes and use her arms and legs to move slowly up Luna's trunk. Finally, she felt ready to make the difficult climb to the

*Julia had to learn how to climb Luna
using ropes and a harness.*

small platform. But halfway up the tree, she made a mistake by looking down.

I could get myself killed, she thought when she saw the ground far below and the platform high above. Frozen in place, she could not climb up and she wasn't sure how to climb down. She closed her eyes and pressed her face against Luna's soft bark. *Don't panic*, she told herself. *Be calm*. Feeling Luna's strength gave Julia the courage to push on.

Soon she reached the platform. A tree-sitter named Shakespeare, whose place she was taking, explained that the support crew would bring food and supplies every three days. He showed her the rope that she would throw down so food could be tied to it and pulled up.

Shakespeare showed her how to collect drinking water. He also explained about using plastic buckets as a bathroom. He tightened the blue tarps that hung over the platform and told Julia not to let them become loose. This was her roof, her only protection against wind, rain, and snow.

As Shakespeare rappelled down the tree, he called one final warning: "Watch out for Climber Dan!"

Climber Dan worked for the Pacific Lumber Company. His job was to bring tree-sitters down from the trees. Using a gun-like device, he would shoot his ropes into the highest branches. Then he would climb above the tree-sitting platform

and drop down onto it. Climber Dan would wrestle tree-sitters to the floor and bind their hands with duct tape. Then he would tie them in a harness and lower them to the ground.

Julia peered down and waved to Almond as he tied her backpack to the supply ropes. It contained a sleeping bag, clothes, two hats, a pair of gloves, a journal, and some food. He gave the signal and she pulled her belongings up to her new home. It was December 10, 1997. Julia Butterfly Hill didn't know it at the time, but her feet would not touch ground for another 738 days.

Supplies are sent up to Julia on the end of a very long rope.

Early the next morning loggers began shouting, "Hey, you stupid tree-hugger!" Julia was startled to hear human voices.

Throughout the night she had heard only the wind blowing through the trees.

"You're coming down today for sure," a logger yelled.

Julia scrambled to the edge of the platform and saw below the tops of three yellow hardhats. One man was busy fastening a thick climbing belt around his waist. It was Climber Dan. He fixed his ropes and attached special spikes to his shoes. He then shot his lead rope high into Luna's upper branches.

But there was a problem. Every time Climber Dan tried to get a firm hold of his lead line, Luna's upper branches, damaged by a lightning strike, decay, and old age, broke under his weight. Climber Dan could not climb above the platform. Three times he tried to obtain a strong guideline. Three times he failed.

Julia smiled with relief and patted Luna's trunk. "We're safe for now."

The following day she was greeted by more angry words. Loggers hammered an eviction notice to Luna's trunk. Julia was breaking the law. Luna was growing on Pacific Lumber property. If she refused to leave private property, she could be arrested for trespassing.

Yet she knew that if she climbed down, Luna would be cut down. There was no one who would take her place during the cold winter weather. She couldn't bear the thought of Luna crashing to the ground and being made into lawn chairs. She was determined to see this through to the end.

Julia whispered, "I will not leave you, Luna, until you're safe."

Living in Luna

What was supposed to be a one-week relief-sit for another tree-sitter became much more. As time passed, Julia found that her childhood experiences had prepared her for the challenge of living in a tree. There isn't a lot of room on a small square platform, yet it felt cozy and familiar to her. It reminded her of the small bunk area in her family's camper.

There was no electricity, which meant no television or computer—things Julia wasn't very attached to in the first place. What she did have was her journal, in which she expressed all her hopes and fears. She wrote hundreds of poems and drew pictures about saving Luna and the forest.

Julia had the company of the animals that lived in and around Luna. Northern flying squirrels provided hours of entertainment. They would land on her platform and scurry to the containers filled with granola and other foods.

Sometimes Julia would leave a few crumbs for the squirrels. She'd laugh as she watched them carry their treasure to higher branches.

At night, squirrel friends were not so entertaining. Squirrels are nocturnal, so their most active time is during the night when Julia tried to sleep. It's difficult to rest when there's a squirrel party on your bed. Julia tried to remember that she was the visitor here and that she must be a good neighbor.

On the morning of January 21, after forty-two days in the tree, she awoke to a terrifying churning sound. Luna's

Julia enjoyed reading and writing during all her free time. She is shown here surrounded by the supplies that helped her survive living in Luna for two years.

Sometimes Julia felt lonely, so she was given a cell phone to contact her family and friends. She also used the phone to tell her ground support about anything she needed. Here, she is being interviewed by a reporter.

branches were whipping wildly about. The loud whirring noise hurt Julia's ears. Frightened and confused, she hugged Luna's trunk with all her strength. *What is it?* Julia frantically thought.

Then she saw a helicopter hovering in the air with its metal blades rotating less than 20 feet (6 meters) from her platform.

The helicopter looked like a giant metal insect threatening Julia and Luna.

Three times the helicopter came dangerously close to the tree. But the Pacific Lumber Company could not frighten her into climbing down. She had stood up to bullies before.

After a while Julia became a celebrity. She had broken the tree-sitting world record, which was ninety days. Newspaper and television reporters interviewed her in person and over the cell phone. It wasn't every day that a twenty-two-year-old woman decides to live in a tree in order to save it from being cut down.

The Pacific Lumber Company was angry. It did not like its logging practices questioned. Julia Butterfly Hill was interfering with its work, and the company was determined to stop her.

But Climber Dan failed to bring her down. Helicopters failed to frighten her down. So during the winter, the Pacific Lumber Company hired security guards to camp out at the base of Luna's trunk. Their job was to stop Julia's crew from bringing her food. Surely, hunger would force her to the ground.

One week passed and she had not received supplies. Three grumpy guards camped out around Luna. Sometimes they called insults to Julia. Other times they tried to bribe her to come down by saying they'd all go out for pizza, but she

Julia told reporters, "I wanted to protect Luna for her sake and for the thousands of people across the country and around the world for whom she has become a symbol of hope, a reminder that we can find peaceful, loving ways to solve our conflicts." [7]

refused. She obtained water by a system set up to collect moisture on the tarps, and she still had a small supply of granola to eat.

During the second week of the stakeout, the guards played loud music at night and blasted air horns. They directed large floodlights at Julia's platform to keep her from sleeping. Although she was very tired, she did not give up.

The president of the Pacific Lumber Company, John Campbell, wrote a letter to Julia's parents, urging them to tell their daughter to come down. Julia's father responded, "If John Campbell thinks he can outwait my daughter, he doesn't know my daughter. Every time her mother and I tried to control her or outwait her on something, we always lost."[8]

Julia's father was right. After two weeks of not being able to bring her supplies, the ground crew came up with an idea. Ten activists arrived at the base of Luna's tree and ran around hooting and hollering.

While the outnumbered guards chased the activists, Julia threw down her supply line. A package was quickly tied to the line and she hoisted her food to the platform. Soon the guards gave up and went home, leaving Julia and Luna to face the winter storms alone.

A Beacon of Light

During a tree-sit, it is customary to hang a beacon of light from a high branch. The light runs on a battery, and at night it shines as a symbol of hope. After Julia had lived up in Luna's branches for over a year, she and Luna had become a symbol of hope for many people, especially children.

Julia's dad, Dale Hill, going to see her during a rally. He was always very supportive of all her efforts.

Schoolchildren from all over the world sent Julia hundreds of letters and pictures every week. The children told her how much they admired what she was doing. They drew pictures of her sitting in Luna. They told her, "Don't give up!"

Julia answered many of these letters. She wrote that each child could make a difference in the world and that Earth needs their protection.

At this point Julia had formed an intense bond with Luna and refused to be relieved from her duty. Julia was afraid another tree-sitter might give up and Luna would be cut down. She promised that she would not leave Luna until the Pacific Lumber Company agreed to change its logging practices.

The Pacific Lumber Company began increasing the rate of clear-cutting the forests surrounding Luna. Day after day, Julia heard the buzz of chainsaws and saw the results of cutting down the forest. This was the most painful part of the tree-sit. It saddened her to watch the destruction of the redwood forest from Luna's high branches.

During her tree-sit, Julia read everything she could on environmental issues and law. She became an expert at giving speeches and interviews over the cell phone. She received an honorary degree from a college. Magazines voted her one of the Most Admired Women of 1998.

The Pacific Lumber Company president, John Campbell

Celebrities like singer Joan Baez, singer Bonnie Raitt, and actor Woody Harrelson came to visit Luna and show their support. At the end of Julia's second year in Luna, an unexpected visitor came to the forest—John Campbell, the president of the Pacific Lumber Company.

The Environmental Protection Agency had recently cited Campbell's company for over three hundred violations of the California State Forest Practice Act. Campbell needed to end

Julia's tree-sit because it brought more attention to the company's practices. He was willing to make a deal.

The Luna Preservation Agreement and Deed of Covenant saved Luna and all the trees within a 200-foot (61-meter) buffer zone.[9] Environmental groups paid the Pacific Lumber company $50,000 for the land. The company then donated the money to Humboldt County College for environmental research.

Some people accused Julia of selling out. But most people felt she was a heroine. By living in Luna's branches for two years, she brought attention to the importance of saving our forests.

Julia had mixed feelings about finally climbing down. She had really missed taking hot showers, sleeping in a bed, and walking on the ground. But she knew she would now miss seeing golden sunrises, the mist-covered valley, and the strength and beauty of Luna.

Julia's hands and feet were stained brown from free-climbing without ropes around Luna's sap-covered branches. She liked to climb barefoot because the sticky sap improved her grip. She had become expert at shifting her weight and choosing which branches would support her. Before she said good-bye to Luna, she wanted one last climb. This time Julia would try to free-climb to the very top.

Julia makes an exhilarating climb to the very top of Luna before she heads down to the ground.

Carefully, Julia climbed above her tree-house home in the sky. At the very top, Julia straddled Luna's highest branch and breathed in the cool December air. She held her arms up to the sky.

Tomorrow, she would climb down and walk with people on the earth for the first time in 738 days. But at this moment she felt more alive and free than ever before. Julia Butterfly Hill

Julia hikes out of the forest with her dad (right) and other supporters.

Here, the ground crew gathers around Julia—she couldn't have done this without them.

found her purpose in life on top of the world, living among the cloudsweepers.

After Julia climbed down, she stood before reporters and said, "Luna is only one tree. We will save her, but we will lose others. The more we stand up and demand change, the more things will improve. I ask myself sometimes whether the destruction has gone too far, whether we can really do anything to save our forests and our planet. And, yet I know that I can't give up. . . . Yes, one person *can* make a difference. Each one of us does."[10]

Important Dates

1974 Julia Hill is born February 18 in the back of a bakery truck in Mount Vernon, Missouri.

1979 She is home-schooled for the next nine years by her parents as the family travels around the country in a camper.

1980 A monarch butterfly lands and remains on her finger while she is hiking in the forest. Her family gives her the nickname Butterfly.

1988 Her family settles in Arkansas. Julia attends public school for the first time.

1996 She has a serious car accident. Her recovery takes over ten months.

1997 She visits Humboldt County, California, to see the redwood forests and volunteers to take a tree-sitter's place in a tree. She climbs a tree named Luna on December 10.

1998 Julia breaks the ninety-day world record for the longest tree-sit. December 10 marks her one-year anniversary in Luna. She is voted one of the Most Admired Women of the year by several magazines.

1999 The Luna Preservation Agreement and Deed of Covenant protects Luna and the surrounding trees. Julia climbs down on December 18 after 738 days living in a redwood tree.

2000 She helps establish the Circle of Life Foundation, dedicated to saving Earth's natural resources. Julia's book, *The Legacy of Luna*, is published.

2001 She settles in Humboldt County, California, where she devotes herself to working on environmental issues.

Notes

1. Trish Rohrer Deitch, "Out on a Limb," *Elle*, March 2000, p. 260.

2. Julia Butterfly Hill, *The Legacy of Luna* (San Francisco: HarperSanFrancisco, 2000), p. 8.

3. Deitch, p. 260.

4. Hill, p. 23.

5. Hill, p. 24.

6. Hill, p. 15.

7. Hill, p. 234.

8. Hill, p. 151.

9. Deitch, p. 260.

10. Hill, p. 238.

Further Reading

BOOKS

Appelbaum, Diana. *Giants in the Land*. Boston: Houghton Mifflin, 1993.

Hill, Julia Butterfly. *The Legacy of Luna: The Story of a Tree, a Woman, and the Struggle to Save the Redwoods*. San Francisco: HarperSanFrancisco, 2000.

Marsh, Carole. *Big Trees! The Redwoods, Giant Sequoias and Kings Canyon National Park*. Peachtree City, GA: Gallopade Publishing Group, 1996.

Mellett, Peter. *Trees: Fantastic Facts*. New York: Lorenz Books, 2000.

Schneider, Bill. *The Tree Giants: The Story of the Redwoods, the World's Largest Trees*. Guilford, CT: Falcon Publishing Company, 1998.

Vieira, Linda. *The Ever-Living Tree: The Life and Times of a Coast Redwood*. New York: Walker and Company, 1995.

WEB SITES

ANCIENT FOREST INTERNATIONAL

www.ancientforests.org

This Web site is dedicated to the protection of ancient forests. It includes maps, trail guides, and scientific information.

CIRCLE OF LIFE FOUNDATION

www.circleoflifefoundation.org

This Web site contains photos, poetry, letters, and up-to-date information on Julia Hill's environmental projects.

SAVE-THE-REDWOODS LEAGUE

www.savetheredwoods.org

Since 1918, the Save-the-Redwoods League has been working to preserve the redwood forests of California. This Web site explains how the league buys redwood forests and places them in protection. It offers links to other Web sites on redwoods.

Index

About the Author

Dawn FitzGerald is a teacher and the author
of four children's biographies. Passionate about the
unsung heroines in history, she was moved by the
challenges Julia Butterfly Hill faced and wanted to
make her story known to young readers. FitzGerald
lives in Ohio with her husband and two children
and enjoys bicycling, reading, and drawing.